Fear
of
Firing

By
Richard S. Deems, Ph.D.

CAREER PRESS
3 Tice Road
P.O. Box 687
Franklin Lakes, NJ 07417
1-800-CAREER-1
201-848-0310 (outside U.S.)
FAX: 201-848-1727

FEAR OF FIRING

ISBN 1-56414-164-0, $12.99

Cover design by A Good Thing, Inc.

Printed in the U.S.A. by Book-mart Press

To order this title by mail, please include price as noted above, $2.50 handling per order, and $1.00 for each book ordered. Send to: Career Press, Inc., 3 Tice Road, P.O. Box 687, Franklin Lakes, NJ 07417.

Or call toll-free 1-800-CAREER-1 (Canada: 201-427-0229) to order using VISA or MasterCard, or for further information on books from Career Press.

Library of Congress Cataloging-in-Publication Data

Deems, Richard S.
    Fear of firing / by Richard S. Deems.
        p.   cm.
    Includes index.
    ISBN 1-56414-164-0 (paper)
    1. Employees--Dismissal of--Handbooks, manuals, etc.   I. Title.
HF5549.5.D55D43   1995
658.3'13--dc20   95-97
                                                                   CIP

Contents

Chapter 7

How do I put the care and control approach to termination into action?

Foreword

This is my third book on the topic of termination and how to fire someone. Sure, I know what you're thinking: "Just what kind of person writes books about how to fire people?"

Really, I'm a fairly decent person. I smile, laugh, help others, pay my taxes, do most of the cooking in my home, use the turn signals on my car, scratch dogs behind the ears, have time to play games with grandkids and things like that. I also know why the bottom line is important, understand P&L sheets and believe in pay for performance. It's just that, back in the 1980s, I kept hearing stories about managers and companies who were mishandling terminations. As a friend said, "There has to be a better way."

"There has to be a way," he continued, "for companies who really do care about their employees to show that they care—even in the termination process." Care. That was important, we all agreed. There was something else that was important. It was important, we heard from those who had to conduct terminations, that they stay in control of the process so that it all went as smoothly as possible.

As we continued to talk and listen, the care and control concept began to emerge.

Our objective? We wanted to be able to steer managers through the termination process so that the company didn't end up in court and the exiting employee wasn't devastated. The guidelines led to workshop handouts, and finally to this book and its accompanying video.

When you show that you and your company care about the exiting employee, you do certain things and you don't do others. When you remain in control of the termination meeting, you do certain things and you don't do others. This book tells you about those things.

Terminations don't have to leave the exiting employees devastated, the remaining employees angry and the company open to lawsuits. When care and control are in place, the manager's effectiveness is increased, remaining employees have regard for their employer and the company's reputation in the marketplace is enhanced.

The two key words are care and control.

Richard S. Deems, Ph.D.

Chapter 1

What do I need to be concerned about?

Chapter 1 objectives

This is "must read" information! After you have read this chapter and completed its exercises, you should be able to:

- ➲ Describe the care and control approach to termination.
- ➲ Identify how many people are really involved in just a single termination.
- ➲ Assess the risk of litigation in any termination.
- ➲ Describe how terminations impact the marketplace.
- ➲ Describe how terminations impact the company's reputation.
- ➲ Discuss your role in a termination and how to keep your thinking clear.

What began in the 1980s is continuing in the 1990s—job terminations. During the 1980s, several million Americans experienced job termination. Some of those terminations were the result of poor performance; others were caused by reorganization and downsizing. It's almost a certainty that several million more will have to deal with job loss before the end of the 1990s.

Because it's now taking place so frequently, termination has become a much-talked-about fact of corporate life. Do it the right way, and there's only minimal workplace disruption. But do it the wrong way, and the company's bottom-line profitability and reputation can suffer.

The care and control approach to termination

The most effective approach when "you have to fire someone" is the care and control approach. When you show that you and your company care about the exiting employee(s), and you remain in *control* of the termination discussion, there is as little disruption as possible.

"Sounds good," you say, "but wait a minute." Your thinking may continue something like this: "Terminations always involve disruption. You can't get away from it. People get upset, their friends wonder what happened, schedules get messed up and somehow the work still needs to get done. What do you mean you can conduct a termination with as little disruption as possible?"

You're right, terminations do result in some disruption. People do get angry, their friends always wonder what happened and all of those other things happen, too, just like you said. But you can conduct terminations in ways that reduce and minimize the disruption. That's what this book is all about.

When you adopt the care and control approach, you set in motion the dynamics for these things to happen:

- The exiting employee can retain his or her dignity and receives assistance in the transition process.

- The exiting employee can leave with regard for the company.

- There is little, if any, risk of litigation.

- The company is regarded by remaining employees as a good place to work.

- The company's reputation in the marketplace even may be enhanced.

Handling a termination goes beyond just doing it in a legally defensible way. Showing that the company cares about exiting employees can take several different forms. Some of them include:

● Planning what you will and will not say.

● Coordinating the logistics so that you're able to give helpful information to the exiting employee during the termination meeting.

● Not embarrassing the exiting employee.

● Not embarrassing remaining employees.

● Scheduling the termination meeting so the exiting employee has time to adjust to the job loss.

● Informing affected work units and company customers, when appropriate.

● Conducting the termination meeting in a professional manner.

Staying in control means just that—demonstrating that you are in control of the termination meeting and staying in control regardless of what happens or what the exiting employee says or does. This can mean:

● Not losing your temper.

● Not arguing about termination decisions.

● Using carefully selected words during the termination meeting.

● Being firm, though caring, in what you say.

● Anticipating the different reactions of the exiting employee and planning how you might respond to them.

● Planning ahead.

● Letting the exiting employee know that you, not the employee, are in control of the meeting.

There are other areas of concern for you to keep in mind as you plan and conduct any termination. It's important that you're aware of them if you are to develop and implement your own care and control approach to termination.

Take a moment...

During a staff meeting, your team leader discusses the need to terminate an employee because of performance. Your team leader knows you've been reading a new book on termination and asks you to describe the care and control approach. Use the space below to describe the care and control approach to termination in your own words.

_____

_____

_____

_____

For every action, there is a reaction

Actions always are followed by reactions. We all know that, but sometimes we forget it. For example, you throw a ball up in the air (the action) and the ball ultimately comes back down (the reaction). But it never comes 100 percent straight down, and to catch it, you have to move.

Now apply this to terminations. You can't just terminate one employee and think that there aren't other dynamics taking place. Even if you terminate someone late on Friday afternoon (the worst time to do it, by the way), there are reactions. Why? Because one single termination affects a lot of other people. This is true whether the termination is performance-based or due to a reorganization or downsizing.

Stop for a moment and think about how many people really are involved in a termination. As an example, let's imagine a 10-year employee who is a supervisor, married and with a family, and whose job is being eliminated due to a downsizing. Here are the other people who also might be involved:

15

The employee	one person
The employee's spouse and children	three people
The employee's work unit	nine people
Friends within the company	20 people, a conservative estimate
Friends within the community	25 people, a conservative estimate
Relatives	15 people, spread nationwide
The spouse's co-workers	15 people, a conservative estimate
The children's close friends/families	15 people, a conservative estimate
Total people involved	**103 people (at a minimum)**

And you thought you were dealing with a single individual!

The sheer number of people involved is part of the reason you need to be so careful in planning and conducting a termination. But there are other reasons, too, which include litigation, marketplace response and company reputation.

Take a moment...

Take some time to make out your own list of how many people can be directly and indirectly involved in a single termination. Think of the last person you may have terminated (or talk with a supervisor or manager who has just had to terminate an employee). Then take this exercise and fill in the appropriate numbers:

Employee's name: _____

Employee's job/title/role: _____

Number of people in the employee's family (include employee, spouse and children): _____

Number of people in the employee's work unit: _____

Estimated number of the exited employee's friends still working within the company: _____

Estimated number of the exited employee's friends within the community: _____

Estimated number of the exited employee's relatives within the community: _____

Estimated number of the spouse's co-workers (if the spouse works): _____

Estimated number of close friends of the exited employee's children: _____

Total people involved: _____

Here's something you can do to remind yourself that for every action there is a reaction. The next time you have to conduct a termination, take time during the planning stage to fill in these numbers. You may be surprised. This exercise provides compelling reasons to plan and conduct the termination with as much care and control as possible.

Litigation

The possibility of litigation exists in any termination. Even if the terminated employee has no valid reason for a suit, the person always can decide to go ahead and file a wrongful-discharge suit anyway. Sometimes the employee is talked into taking legal action. For years, one of the fastest growing legal specialties was that of employment plaintiff lawyers. It's still a large and typically very aggressive field.

Even responding to a possible suit costs the company time and money. Some human-resources managers have estimated that just the cost of researching the situation and responding to a letter of intent to file suit can be as high as $8,000 in time and external legal fees. Defending an actual suit can cost six figures.

If an employee believes he or she has been discriminated against because of age, gender, ethnic origin, disability, religion or some other parameter, that person may have a viable case. In some states, laws enable a terminated employee to seek damages from his or her immediate supervisor if the ex-employee believes he or she was not managed correctly.

There is no way to completely avoid the risk of litigation. Sometimes ex-employees are so angry that they file a suit regardless of whether or not they have a viable case. However, when you follow the recommendations of this book and use the care and control approach to termination, you greatly reduce the risk of a lawsuit.

Take a moment...

Now, while you're thinking about it, start a new file and call it something like "Fired!" or "Litigation." Then, as you read newspaper and magazine articles about employee lawsuits in your geographic area, clip them out, write the date of the article in the margin and put them in your new file. Periodically review your file. You'll increase your insight into the kinds of employee-related lawsuits that are being filed and that catch the local media's attention.

Marketplace response

As you've already realized, there are a lot of people involved in a single termination. If you have an angry exiting employee who's leaving (for whatever reason) without any regard for the company, you've set in motion some dynamics that can hurt business. For example, let's imagine you're part of a company that makes widgets, and you are going to downsize by 200 employees. Multiply that number by 103 others who are directly or indirectly affected, and you come up with at least 20,600 people who are affected in one way or another because of that downsizing.

Do it the wrong way, and you can have more than 20,000 people who may or may not ever buy another widget your company produces. Those same people also will be talking to their circles of friends about the poor way in which your company let people go. And these people have friends and relatives all across the country who can be expected to talk about what happened. Pretty soon, there can be thousands of people nationwide who respond by buying somebody else's widgets.

There also is the issue of media attention. If an angry exiting employee or family member calls the local media and starts talking about even a single termination, the media may give it some attention. If there's a downsizing involved, the media is even more likely to report it, particularly if there are negative feelings from exiting employees and their families.

For some companies that have received negative media attention, it has taken several years to regain their stature in the marketplace. They were the lucky ones; other companies never regained it.

Fortunately, the reverse also is true. Help employees leave with regard for the company, and you can have thousands of people talking about the great way in which your company treats its people. Do it the right way, and you can be rewarded with lots of people outside your company who have a new sense of product loyalty—and people on the inside who believe your company is "a great place to work."

Company reputation

Employees talk about companies just like managers talk about employees. And companies get reputations as being good places to work or places to stay away from.

If your company gets the reputation of being a good place to work, it will have its pick of top candidates when positions open. It also will be the place people go for their entry-level jobs because of its reputation for treating its employees fairly. The real payoff comes when the company needs specialized people.

When the ABC Corporation needed to add to its MIS Department, it required top-level systems analysts and end-user consultants. A well-placed ad resulted in a sizable pool of applicants, and the company was able to add the necessary people without compromising its goal of hiring only top-notch and experienced specialists.

The DEF Corporation, on the other hand, had just the opposite experience. Known as a company who "chews them up and spits them out," the company had a similar need to add to its MIS Department. But their reputation as an employer hurt them as they tried to recruit new people. Even though they were paying more than the ABC Corporation, they didn't attract the same level of candidates. Finally, they were forced to recruit in neighboring cities where their reputation wasn't as widely known. The result: Their costs of hiring were considerably higher than other local companies, and the level of their candidates was lower than they'd hoped for.

The way in which a company terminates people contributes to its overall reputation as an employer. A company that terminates people fairly and with regard for the exiting employees' reactions gains the reputation of being "a company that cares about its people." But one that does it carelessly gets the reputation of being "a company to stay away from."

A manager can say, "I care about our people," but his or her actions must support those words. If that manager terminates employees on a Friday afternoon for little or no cause, provides minimal or no assistance and conducts the termination in ways that embarrass the exiting as well as the remaining employees, it doesn't take long for people to realize that words and actions don't match. The manager's and the company's reputations both suffer.

Employees really talk about their company every time there's a termination. If they believe their company has terminated an employee fairly, whatever the reason, they will maintain their morale and productivity. But the reverse also is true: If the remaining employees believe someone has been let go unfairly or in a careless manner, morale will suffer, pride in the company will decline and productivity and quality will drop. It's that simple.

Companies that will enjoy healthy reputations in the year 2001 are those that are following the care and control approach to termination today!

Self-check

Indicate whether you think each of the following statements is True or False. Suggested answers appear in the section beginning on page 109.

T/F Terminations that result in angry exiting employees do not hurt business.

T/F When employees believe another employee has been treated fairly, their morale and productivity drop very little, if at all.

T/F Product loyalty can be enhanced by using the care and control approach to termination.

T/F Negative media attention can hurt business.

T/F Companies with a reputation for treating their employees fairly also enjoy the reputation of being a good place to work.

T/F Words such as "we care about our people" must be supported by actions that back them up.

T/F The way in which a company terminates people does not contribute to its overall reputation as an employer.

T/F Employees talk about their companies.

T/F The public forms opinions of companies.

T/F Conducting terminations using the care and control approach can enhance a company's reputation in the marketplace.

Keeping your own head straight

"Okay," you say, "you've convinced me. I believe we can have a care and control approach to termination." But you pause a bit. Why the hesitation?

Finally you admit: "It's just that it's hard to think that letting someone go is a way of showing them that we care."

You're right. But as you'll see, there are many ways to overlay the termination process with words and actions that show you and the company do care. That's important, because occasionally having to conduct a termination is a necessary part of your job.

Sometimes the termination is necessary because the employee's poor performance is costing the company money. Or a downsizing may be needed if the company is to stay profitable and competitive. In some cases, though not often, a termination is simply the end result of someone not doing a very good job of managing someone else.

If you're going to use the care and control approach to termination, you need to have your own head on straight and understand why terminations need to happen and how you fit into the termination process.

Understand your own role in the process

Regardless of the reason for the termination, your primary role is to make certain that it takes place with as little disruption as possible. This means you:

● Implement the care and control approach to termination.

● Follow the guidelines presented in the next chapter.

● Plan and prepare yourself to deal with all possible employee reactions.

● Complete the necessary follow-through responsibilities.

Or to put it another way, your role is to enhance your company's reputation in the marketplace.

If you are the decision-maker in a termination or you have to recommend whose jobs are eliminated in a downsizing, then to enhance your company's reputation, you must be certain that the termination is:

● Fair.

● Justified.

● Handled correctly.

● Conducted so your company is not put at risk.

Don't worry—you won't be left to do all this by yourself. We'll show you how in the following chapters.

Part of your overall role as a manager or supervisor is to make sure your company runs effectively and efficiently, and sometimes that requires terminations. But that doesn't relegate you to the role of a monster. Your role is simply to carry out each and every termination with as little disruption as possible. Even if you don't agree with the decision to terminate, your role still is to plan and conduct that termination with a care and control approach.

At times, personal feelings will make it more difficult for you to conduct a care and control termination. But personal feelings sometimes must be set aside.

Remember—it's a business decision.

Understand business decisions

Terminations are prompted by decisions based upon basic business principles. In the case of a termination due to poor performance, the business decision is simply that the company can't afford an employee who is not meeting performance expectations in that particular position. The poor-performing employee may be affecting co-workers, whose performance also may begin to drop. The poor-performing employee may be putting users of the company's products at risk, simply because of inadequate quality or unsafe working conditions.

When an employee is not performing up to standards, it usually means he or she is not suited for that particular position. If the employee has been given the opportunity to improve performance and doesn't, then the termination actually does a favor for the exiting employee. This is especially so with companies that choose to help the exiting employee by providing outplacement services, career counseling or retraining.

Downsizings also are based upon business decisions. For whatever reason, a company must reorganize or reduce costs. Since a company's biggest percentage of costs comes from employee salaries, that is where it typically will begin to economize.

Often a downsizing is the only action that will enable a company to remain competitive and to stay in business.

The decade of the '90s will see a lot of economic change and, in part, that economic change will translate into terminations. Performance expectations will tend to be higher, and people who are not suited for their jobs will increasingly receive lateral moves or be terminated. Some companies will need to downsize in one division while they increase the number of employees in another.

In any case, remember to keep your own head straight as you plan and conduct those terminations. When you do that—when you exercise care and control—you serve your company well and you do its exiting employees a favor, too.

Take a moment...

You've dealt with a lot of information and material up to this point. Before going any further, stop and think about your own role in the termination process. Use the space below to write down your thoughts:

_____

_____

_____

_____

Now go back and review what you have written, underlining words and phrases that show you are using the care and control approach.

"I have to fire someone!" You probably wouldn't be reading this book unless, sometime in the near future, you expect to face that task. Remember that the most effective approach is the one that shows you and your company care about the exiting employee and the one that puts you in control of the meeting. Taken together, those two things can ensure that there will be as little disruption as possible.

And that has been your goal from the start!

Chapter 1 review

Indicate whether you think each of the following statements is True or False.

T/F The goal is to conduct every termination so there is as little disruption as possible.

T/F The most effective approach to termination is the care and control approach.

T/F There are a lot more people involved in any termination than just the employee being terminated.

T/F There is always the risk of litigation with any termination.

T/F The care and control approach to termination reduces the risk of litigation.

T/F Helping exiting employees leave with regard for the company helps in the marketplace response.

T/F How a company terminates employees affects its reputation.

T/F Whatever your role in the termination process, it is important that you carry out the termination in a care and control manner.

If you marked each statement True, congratulations! These are the areas of concern that make it important to have a care and control approach to termination and that result in as little disruption as possible!

Notes

Chapter 2

What are the guidelines for a care and control approach to termination?

Chapter 2 objectives

After reading this chapter and completing the interactive exercises, you should be able to explain the importance of each of the eight guidelines that are part of the care and control approach to termination:

1. Show that the company cares.

2. Stay in control.

3. Don't socialize.

4. Don't argue.

5. Avoid embarrassing the exiting employee.

6. Avoid embarrassing the remaining employees.

7. Always have at least two people present.

8. Protect your company's customers.

Fact One: Terminations result in disruption.

Fact Two: Try as you might, there is nothing you can do to change Fact One.

Fact Three: There are, however, eight guidelines you can follow to ensure that the terminations you conduct result in as little disruption as possible!

No matter what the termination situation, when you follow these guidelines, you:

● Reduce the chances for error, litigation and bad press.

- Increase opportunities for the company to enhance its reputation in the marketplace.

- Show that your company has genuine care and concern for its employees—even those who must exit, for whatever reason.

Here are the guidelines:

1. Show that the company cares

When you take the time and make the effort to show that the company cares about the soon-to-be-exiting employee, you set in motion an action that has some very positive reactions:

- The company's reputation in the marketplace is now enhanced.

- The company's reputation as an employer is enhanced.

- There is much less risk of litigation.

- The morale and productivity of remaining employees remains high.

- It becomes easier to recruit top candidates to fill any vacancies.

- The employee can exit with regard for the company.

What is meant by the "care" approach? It means carefully choosing what you say and doing nothing that demeans or embarrasses the exiting employee. It means speaking, not out of spite, but because you want to help the exiting employee be successful in this transition. And it means being sensitive to the reactions of the exiting employee and the remaining employees.

2. Stay in control

Nothing is gained if, during the termination meeting, you lose control of the meeting or of yourself. Care is followed by control. The two go together. One is ineffective without the other.

Staying in control means following the guidelines presented in this chapter. It also means planning and preparing for whatever contingency may occur. It means that, whatever happens, you remain in control of the meeting and the exiting process.

3. Don't socialize

The termination meeting is not a time to ask about the family, make small talk about what the employee is wearing or even mention the weather. Even though you may be uncomfortable as the person enters the room—or the whole setting is uncomfortable for you—socializing is not called for in this situation. Terminating a person is serious business for both you and the soon-to-be-exiting employee, and getting right to the point of the meeting will serve to underscore that.

"I thought Jack was pretty rude when we fired Tom last week," Angel reported. "Tom walked in, Jack said thanks for being on time, introduced me and then asked Tom to sit down. The next thing I knew, Jack was talking about Tom's performance…"

"As I think back on it," Angel continued, "it was clean, professional and really worked out best. Tom knew from the beginning that this was a serious meeting, and Jack stayed in control."

Take a moment...

Here are five statements that might be used at the beginning of a termination meeting. Which three are the most effective?

1. "Thank you for being prompt, Tom. I believe you know Angel from human resources. Let's get right to the purpose of our meeting…"

2. "Hello, Tom. Let me introduce Angel who is our human-resources manager. Since you're no doubt wondering about the reason for our meeting, let's sit down and begin…"

3. "Hi, Tom—good to see you again. How's your wife liking her new job? Oh yes, do you know Angel from human

resources? Angel, why don't you take a few minutes and tell Tom about how you got your job here..."

4. "Hello, Tom. Sit down. This is Angel from human resources. She's here to tell you that you're fired."

5. "Thank you, Tom, for being prompt—I appreciate that. Please sit down at the table with Angel and me. I believe you know Angel from human resources. Tom, I appreciate your comments about the weather, but our meeting today is a very serious one, so let's move on to why we're here..."

Hopefully you picked statements 1, 2 and 5. Now think of the upcoming termination you need to conduct. Use the space below to write down what you might say as the soon-to-be-exiting employee arrives for the meeting.

_____

_____

_____

_____

4. Don't argue

After hearing the words that their employment is terminated, some employees will want to talk about why. They will want to discuss it and try to change the mind of whomever they are talking with. In other words, they will want to argue.

The termination discussion is not the time to get caught up in any kind of argument with the exiting employee about anything. If the employee begins to argue, you must act like a broken record and continue to say something like, "John, the decision has been made, and it's final. There is no sense in arguing with me about it."

Sometimes those conducting the termination meeting need to continue with something like, "John, I'm not going to argue with you about the decision. It's been made, and it's final. What I want to do now is review the next steps with you..."

Sometimes it has to be said over and over again.

"When Bev began to argue," Jon recalled, "I thought to my-self—well, it's downhill from here. But instead, Shirley leaned into the table, looked Bev square in the eyes and said quietly, 'Beverly, the decision has been made and is final. We're not here to discuss it, but only to inform you of the decision. Please let me go on with the meeting.'"

Jon recounted how Shirley stayed in control all the time. "Every time Bev would begin to argue," Jon noted, "Shirley would quietly interrupt and say the same thing. Finally, Bev sat back and just listened."

If you allow yourself to argue with the exiting employee, you have lost control of the meeting. You also have lost out on the opportunity to show that the company cares. Once you lose control, you may or may not be able to regain it. Even worse, in the heat of the argument, you may say something that the exiting employee later can use against you or the company in court.

Take a moment...

What kinds of statements can you use with a person who wants to argue with you about the termination decision? Use the space below to write down several that you can use later:

_____

_____

_____

_____

5. Avoid embarrassing the exiting employee

Just as not arguing with the exiting employee keeps you in control, not embarrassing the exiting employee shows that you and your company care. This means doing everything you can to make it easy on the employee who will be or just has been terminated. That translates into several actions:

● First, it means conducting the meeting in a room that the employee can enter and exit without a great deal of exposure, such as a private office with a door that can be closed and where the discussion will not be overheard by others.

● Second, it means planning for the employee to leave the workplace without embarrassment. Having an armed security guard walk the employee through the main office to the front door while other employees watch simply doesn't work. Whatever it takes, do all you can to spare the exiting employee embarrassment.

● Third, it means phrasing the announcement to remaining employees in a way that avoids embarrassing the terminated individual. If the exiting employee worked with outside customers, be cautious when you announce the change in who will be handling their accounts.

When you do all you can to spare the terminated person undue embarrassment, you show that you are in control and that you and your company care.

6. Avoid embarrassing the remaining employees

The care approach also means being sensitive to the reactions of remaining employees. Just as it's important not to embarrass the exiting employee, it's also critical that you avoid making your remaining employees uncomfortable.

"It was terrible," Ann reported. "We were all standing at the elevator when Hank approached Susan." Ann continued as she described how, in front of Susan's co-workers, Hank proceeded to fire her. "Just like that," Ann added, "and then he turned and walked away as if nothing had happened. Susan was devastated, and the rest of us were really mad. That's when we all went to see the company president."

It doesn't have to be that way.

For terminations to take place with as little disruption as possible, you must follow this guideline: Avoid embarrassing other employees. This can translate into:

- Conducting the meeting where other employees won't hear what is being said.

- Arranging for the employee's exit so a minimum of remaining employees are involved or aware.

- Making arrangements for the exiting employee to retrieve his or her personal belongings without embarrassment to themselves or others.

- Choosing your words carefully as you notify remaining employees of the employee's exit.

When you avoid embarrassing remaining employees, you not only stay in control, but you continue to show that your company is one that cares about its people. And that adds to its reputation of being a "good place to work."

Take a moment...

Think about your work setting, your company's culture and the termination you will be conducting. Then note the information that's specific to your situation in the spaces provided:

- The office that provides the most privacy for the termination discussion and the least amount of embarrassment for the terminated employee and remaining employees is:

_____

_____

- The least embarrassing way for the terminated employee to leave the premises is:

_____

_____

● The most appropriate care and control approach for notifying remaining employees is:

_____

_____

● The most appropriate care and control approach for notifying company customers is:

_____

_____

● Other procedures I can follow that will avoid embarrassing the exiting employee are:

_____

_____

7. Always have at least two people present

There are several reasons why it's important to have more than one manager present during a termination discussion:

● There is always a witness to what was, and what was not, said or done during the meeting. This can be very important if, later, the discussion is called into question or the termination decision ends up going to court.

● If the person in charge of conducting the meeting experiences a mental block (and it sometimes happens), another person usually can pick up with the right words.

● It's less easy for the terminated employee to argue, become angry, or even resort to becoming physically aggressive if at least two company representatives are present.

So who are these two people?

The person conducting the termination meeting should be the employee's immediate supervisor or manager. The second person can be another supervisor or manager who has related with the employee from time to time, or it may be a representative from the human resources department (or both). If your company has a human resources department, those people usually are trained and skilled in assisting with the termination process.

Whoever is chosen as the second person, that individual needs to be apprised of the decision-making process for the termination, and the two people should review beforehand who will say what.

Even for terminations due to a downsizing, two people representing the company must be present.

Take a moment...

Use the space below to describe your company's policy about who conducts the termination discussion and who the two people present should be:

_____

_____

_____

_____

8. Protect your company's customers!

This means that, if you have an employee who isn't performing up to standards, something needs to be done. If progressive discipline hasn't worked, and the employee has been given the chance and help to improve performance, termination needs to follow. It's as simple as that.

Otherwise, your company's customers may get an inferior product, its cost may be unnecessarily high, or it may be delayed getting to the marketplace. Remember, your task is to satisfy the company's customers.

Sometimes companies need to reorganize and downsize in order to remain competitive—to increase efficiency, keep costs in line or take advantage of new technology. Again, their task is to satisfy their customers.

When you do things right, and remaining employees believe the company has treated the exiting employee fairly, your company will enjoy the reputation of treating its people well—and it will be easier for people to buy from you!

If the terminated employee dealt directly with your company's customers, you must protect them by informing them directly of the change. A personal phone call is more effective than a letter and will build rapport and trust between supplier and customer.

"I really appreciated the phone call when my bank downsized," Sam said. "One of the officers called and told me about the reorganization," he continued, "then she told me who would now be my main contact. I know these things happen, and they kept my business by letting me know personally rather than leaving me to find out the next time I called."

What worked for Sam can work for your company's customers, too!

Chapter 2 review

Here are each of the eight guidelines for the care and control approach to termination. Under each one, write down what it means to you:

1. Show that the company cares.

_____

_____

_____

2. Stay in control.

_____

_____

_____

3. Don't socialize.

_____

_____

_____

4. Don't argue.

_____

_____

_____

5. Avoid embarrassing the exiting employee.

_____

_____

_____

6. Avoid embarrassing the remaining employees.

_____

_____

_____

7. Always have at least two people present.

_____

_____

_____

8. Protect your company's customers.

_____

_____

_____

Notes

Chapter 3

How do I prepare for the termination discussion?

Chapter 3 objectives

After reading this chapter and completing the interactive exercises, you should be able to:

➲ Discuss how to adequately review the reasons for a termination.

➲ Identify the best time to schedule the termination meeting.

➲ Write out a script of what you will say at the meeting.

➲ Coordinate logistics for the termination meeting.

➲ Plan for the follow-through activities.

A termination planning guide detailing these and other key termination activities is included in the back of this book.

A termination is not something to undertake on a whim or the spur of the moment. There are too many people involved and too many dynamics taking place to haphazardly decide to fire or lay off someone without adequate planning and preparation. After all, if you terminate someone the wrong way, your company—and you—can end up in court.

Or your company can lose business...or its valuable reputation in the marketplace.

There are five basic planning steps that should take place before any termination meeting, whether it is a termination due to poor performance or the result of a downsizing. These steps are:

● Review the reasons for the termination.

● Schedule the termination meeting.

● Prepare your script.

● Coordinate the logistics.

● Plan for follow-through.

Here's how to plan a termination meeting that shows you and your company care about its people—and that keeps you in control of the event.

Review the reasons for the termination

Take time to review the reasons for the termination so it's clear in your mind that all basic guidelines for good human resources management have been followed. Also check to make certain that all company policies regarding termination have been followed. This ultimately saves the company time and money and shows that the company does indeed care about its employees.

Terminations due to performance

In the case of termination due to poor performance, you need to make certain that all documentation is in place:

● Make certain that all incidents of below-standard performance have been noted in specific and measurable terms and that it's clear that performance standards have not been met on several occasions.

● Make certain that there is verifiable indication that the employee understood the performance expectations throughout the progressive disciplinary actions.

● Make certain that there is some form of verification that the employee understood the consequences of not meeting those expectations throughout the progressive disciplinary actions.

● Make certain that there have been opportunities for the employee to improve performance over a reasonable period of time and that they've been clearly documented.

● Make certain that documentation of all meetings between the employee and his or her supervisor or manager are complete, with dates and signatures by the appropriate people, and that it's clear all procedures listed in your company's human resources policy manual have been followed.

If you believe that the existing documentation is not sufficient to warrant termination, or there is little or no documentation at all, you're probably better off postponing the termination. Delaying a termination because documentation is insufficient to support it ultimately saves the company time and money.

When the XYZ Corporation decided to terminate Karen because of poor performance, the manager and supervisor reviewed the documentation file. The first notation had been made more than three months earlier, and the summary report of the meeting with Karen identified the performance expectations, what would be done to help her meet those expectations and what the consequences would be if the expectations were not met. Karen and her supervisor both had signed the report. There were other brief notes on the supervisor's efforts to provide help for Karen and on several meetings Karen had with her supervisor—and reports that also had been signed by both. The final note indicated that the performance expectations had not been met in the allotted time and that Karen understood the consequences. After reviewing the file and checking to see that they had complied with all of their company policies, the manager and supervisor were ready to schedule the termination meeting.

Self-check

Read the XYZ Corporation case study again. In the space below, list the six actions taken by Karen's supervisor and manager that followed the care and control approach to termination. Suggested answers appear in the section beginning on page 109.

1. _____

2. _____

3. _____

4. _____

5. _____

6. _____

Termination due to downsizing

A termination due to a downsizing requires a different kind of documentation review. Instead of reviewing a progressive-discipline record, you need to stop and ensure that the criteria established by the company for the job elimination have been followed consistently throughout the affected work units. Using one set of criteria for one department and a different set for another is not always viewed as a fair employment practice. Instead, whatever formula or criteria the company uses to identify those whose jobs will be eliminated must be applied consistently throughout all work units affected by the downsizing. And those criteria cannot be based upon age, gender, disability or national origin, among other parameters.

One way to find out if age, gender, disability or ethnic origin might have been involved in selecting people for job elimination is to develop and review two profiles. The first is a profile by age group, management level, gender, disability and ethnic origin for the company as a whole and for each affected work unit prior to the downsizing. The second profile, using the same categories, is for the whole company and each affected work unit after the proposed downsizing. A quick comparison of the two profiles can show if there is any reason to suspect bias in the selection of those whose jobs will be eliminated.

For example, if prior to the downsizing, the ABC Corporation had a work force comprised of 17 percent females over age 40 and, after the downsizing, it would have a work force of only nine percent females over age 40, it could be said that age and gender bias were involved in selecting those whose jobs were eliminated. However, if after the downsizing, the ABC Corporation would have a work force comprised of 17.7 percent females over age 40, it would appear that no age and gender bias were involved in the determination.

If you believe that the profile comparisons are not sufficient to protect the company, you should bring this information to the attention of the right decision-maker.

Self-check

Below is an age/gender profile for the ABC Corporation *prior* to and *after* a proposed downsizing.

At what points might the profiles indicate that the company showed some bias in selecting people for job elimination?

Female employees by age group	Before	After
Age 18-20	5.7%	7.2%
Age 20-29	16.9%	38.1%
Age 30-39	29.7%	29.4%
Age 40-49	27.7%	13.9%
Age 50-59	17.9%	11.4%
Age 60-65	2.1%	0.0%

It appears that ABC Corporation may have shown female bias in the determination of job eliminations for all age groups over 40 because of the drastic decrease in percent of females working after the downsizing.

Schedule the termination meeting

The timing of the termination meeting is very important. When you practice the care and control approach to termination, you schedule the termination meeting so that:

● The exiting employee has time to begin the adjustment before the end of the workday and before the weekend.

● You can personally notify remaining employees and monitor employee reactions.

● You can notify other employee units (as appropriate) and notify company customers (when applicable).

The most common time to terminate employees is Friday, late afternoon. However, this is the absolute worst time to conduct a termination meeting. It does not show that the company cares, and a Friday afternoon termination eliminates your control of the event. Why? Here are three major reasons:

1. If you terminate on a Friday afternoon, you give the exiting employee very little time to adjust to the job loss before the weekend. Without that adjustment period, the exiting employee typically has not really begun to deal with his or her anger. The employee will talk with others over the weekend, and you can count on some friend saying something like, "I know this attorney..."

2. When you terminate someone on Friday afternoon, the remaining employees don't have much time to talk about it—or they may not have even heard about it when they leave the building. As the word gets out, employees will talk to each other on the phone over the weekend. You may or may not have a problem come Monday morning—but you certainly have no control over what takes place. But if you terminate earlier in the week, you can observe the reactions of remaining employees, and if a problem begins to develop, you can deal with it right away.

3. If you terminate on a Friday afternoon, you have little time to notify others who may be affected, such as

customers and other work units. You run the risk of a key customer finding out about the termination through rumor, or worse, from someone who is angry over what took place.

If Friday afternoon is the worst time to schedule a termination, is there a best time to terminate? Yes.

Over the years, it consistently has been shown that earlier in the week and usually earlier in the day works best. This gives the exiting employee time to adjust before the first weekend, allows remaining employees to discuss and react to the termination, enables managers to deal with any problems that may arise and, when relevant, provides time for customers and other employee groups to be notified.

Just how early in the week? Monday, Tuesday and Wednesday all work well. The key is to plan so you can follow the guidelines of the care and control approach to termination (see Chapter 2). How early in the day? Early can mean 8 a.m., 9 a.m. or mid-morning, but preferably before noon. If the termination "just has to wait" until after lunch, then it needs to take place before 2 p.m. If you wait later than mid-afternoon, you can wait until the next morning, which puts you back in control and shows that you and the company care about its people.

What if the situation is immediate, because of what might be called gross misconduct? Gross misconduct is a special situation and is discussed in Chapter 6.

The office of the employee's manager typically is the best place in which to conduct the termination meeting. Conference rooms and other settings can be used when necessary. What's important is that the meeting place is private, that the exiting employee won't be embarrassed in front of others and that remaining employees won't overhear the discussion.

Make sure that a second person (another supervisor or manager, or a representative from the human-resources department) can be present and that all necessary materials will be ready. Check to see that the employee isn't taking vacation on the target day. Timing is very important for downsizings.

Take a moment...

Use the space below to write down three reasons why it is best to terminate early in the week and early in the day.

_____

_____

_____

_____

_____

Prepare your script

Having a script will help you conduct the termination meeting with care and control. As you take the time to think through what you will say and how you will say it, you can focus on words that show the company cares.

You also can plan what you might say if the person argues or becomes angry. Many managers find it helpful to write out what they plan to say and to go over their script several times. They don't read their script word-for-word during the actual termination, but the preparation readies them for just about any kind of scenario.

"It keeps me in control," Mick reported. "Each time I have to terminate someone or assist in a termination, I take time to write out what I want to say. I don't have a standard script, and I don't want one, either. I don't want to sound canned. And besides, the best way for me to show that the company cares is to treat each situation as unique. It helps."

As you prepare your script, anticipate the terminated employee's possible reactions, and think through how best to respond. Do you think the employee might argue? What if the employee just sits there and stares into space? What if the employee cries? Anticipate each of these reactions, then prepare your own script to deal with them using the care and control approach guidelines.

Two sample scripts are included in Chapter 4.

Take a moment...

Keeping in mind the guidelines from Chapter 2, use the space below to write a brief script for conducting a termination meeting using the care and control approach:

_____

_____

_____

_____

_____

_____

_____

_____

_____

Coordinate logistics

There are many details to take care of when planning and conducting a termination. It's not as easy as just sitting down in a room somewhere and telling a person that his or her employment is terminated. When you follow the care and control approach, it's important that all the logistics are taken care of prior to the day of the termination. This includes:

● The termination has been reviewed and approved. You have reviewed the documentation and believe that the termination is justified and that all company policies have been followed.

● The room has been scheduled. Either the manager's office or some other appropriate room that provides privacy will be available at the designated time.

● The exiting employee will be on the job. The employee will be available to meet and will not be absent due to vacation or off-site work assignment.

- A second person is available and scheduled to come to the meeting. Always have at least two people present; the second person can be a representative from human resources or another supervisor or manager who relates in some capacity to the soon-to-be-exiting employee.

- Your script has been prepared and reviewed with the second person. Prepare what you are going to say, then review it with the second person to be present. Anticipate how the employee may react and how you will respond.

- A letter summarizing the termination and the available company assistance will be ready at the time of the meeting. Check with your human resources department to make sure that a letter summarizing company assistance will be ready to give the exiting employee during the termination meeting.

- Options for the exiting employee to retrieve personal belongings are approved. Identify the best way for the employee to retrieve his or her personal belongings and review it with the appropriate managers.

"I didn't realize so many things had to be taken care of," Hank remarked. "This is my first termination—well, not my first, but the first time I did it with such care and control. Your suggestions and the termination planning guide were a big help," Hank added, as he and the senior human resources coordinator reviewed the earlier termination.

"Well," Beth responded, "we didn't always do it this way. But we learned that taking the extra time to plan helps everyone in the long run." Then, smiling, she added, "And, yes, we learned some things the hard way, too..."

The detailed termination planning guide at the end of this book is designed to help you complete your preparation and co-ordinate all of the logistics.

Plan for follow-through

The termination process isn't over when the exiting employee leaves the building. There are several follow-through activities that still need to take place. These are important enough to be discussed in more detail in Chapter 5. As you go through your termination-planning process, just be certain that you include the time and resources to complete the necessary follow-through.

Chapter 3 review

Suggested answers appear in the section beginning on page 109.

1. List the five basic planning steps for any termination meeting:

_____

_____

_____

_____

_____

_____

2. Mark the following items True or False:

T/F 1. Documentation of poor performance is no longer necessary before terminating an employee.

T/F 2. A downsizing that eliminates all employees over age 50 is good business.

T/F 3. The best time to terminate someone is early in the week and early in the day.

T/F 4. There are fewer problems if you terminate someone late on Friday afternoon.

T/F 5. Normally, the best place to conduct a termination meeting is in the immediate manager's private office.

T/F 6. There are several follow-through activities to complete after the termination discussion is over.

3. List three logistical items that must be coordinated:

_____

_____

_____

Notes

Chapter 4

How do I conduct the termination meeting?

Chapter 4 objectives

After reading this chapter and completing the interactive exercises, you should be able to:

➲ State the purpose of the meeting.

➲ Guide and control the discussion.

➲ Discuss the benefits and assistance the employee will receive.

➲ Assist the employee in leaving the premises.

➲ Document the termination meeting using the care and control approach to termination.

Planning ultimately gives way to the actual doing—carrying out and conducting the termination meeting. The previous chapters on planning the termination meeting are important, and you will conduct the meeting with more confidence (and fewer problems) if you've already read them.

Your goal is to conduct the termination so there is as little disruption as possible. When you use the care and control approach to termination, the result is just that.

The five steps of the termination meeting

There is a normal pattern to the termination meeting that consists of five steps. When you follow these steps and are prepared for each one, the meeting moves more smoothly. You're prepared for each of several reactions by the employee, and the meeting does not need to take a long time. Usually, a 10- to 15-minute meeting is sufficient.

Step 1. State the purpose of the meeting

When the employee enters the office, greet the person, ask him or her to sit down, and introduce the employee to the second manager (often a representative from the human resources department). Then state the purpose of the meeting. Remember, this is not a time for socializing or chit-chat. This is a very serious meeting, and the most effective way to show that the company cares is to get right to the meeting's agenda. You can say something like:

"Roy, we've talked about your performance for the past two months. The company has provided some extra training and time for you to improve your performance. However, your performance has not met our agreed-upon standards, and our meeting today is to inform you of your termination from the ABC Corporation and what the company will do to help you in your transition."

That's all that needs to be said. You don't begin with idle chit-chat, talk about the weather or ask how the kids are. Instead, you get right to the point—that this meeting has been called to inform the employee of his or her termination and, depending on the company, to tell the employee how the company will help in the transition to a new job.

If the termination is due to a downsizing, the statement is somewhat different:

"Roy, as you know, the company has been involved in a number of cost-cutting efforts in order to remain competitive. Because of a reorganization, there will be 15 jobs eliminated, and our meeting today is to tell you that your job is one of them. We also want to tell you what the company will do to help you in the adjustment and to find a new position."

Again, there is no chit-chat or small talk. What works best is to get right to the point of the meeting. The meeting will proceed more effectively when you begin by stating the purpose of the meeting with care and control, and then continue.

One *critical* word of caution: This is not the time to express your own thoughts about the termination! It will not help the exiting employee—or the company or yourself—if you try to small-talk the situation and say something like, "Well, I don't agree with this, but I have to do what the company tells me..." You may not agree with the decision, but if it is your task to carry it out, do so with care and control, and omit your own personal feelings.

Take a moment...

In the space below, write down three reasons why it's best to begin the discussion by stating the purpose of the meeting.

_____

_____

_____

Step 2. Guide and control the discussion

Your task now is to guide and control the remainder of the meeting. Of course, you let the person ask questions. Of course, you try to answer them as clearly as possible. But you do not let yourself enter into an argument with the employee. And you stay in control of all that happens.

If the termination is due to poor performance, the employee may want to argue the point and claim that he or she has met expectations. You must be prepared: Have the summary reports and other documentation on hand, with dates and times of the meetings and what was said by whom. You can continue to show that the company cares by saying something like:

"Roy, here are the reports of your previous meetings with your manager. The notes indicate that you two discussed how progress was not being made. And here are your production reports, which you signed, that show you have not met the expectations that were laid out."

If the person wants to argue about the decision, you sometimes need to be a broken record and continue to repeat, "Roy, the decision has been made, and it won't be changed. Let's move on with our meeting so we can discuss what the company will be providing to help you in your transition..."

If the employee begins to get angry, you need to remain in control. Remember that a person who responds with anger is just trying to gain control of the situation. That's not what you want to happen. You can say something like:

"Roy, please sit down and control yourself. Getting angry isn't going to change the decision. Arguing isn't going to change the decision. Please let me continue with our meeting and explain how the company will handle your exit."

Chapter 6 has specific information on how to handle a number of "what if" situations, including those in which the employee cries, gets angry, doesn't say anything, insists on seeing your boss or the CEO, won't leave the building or threatens to become physical.

The key to a successful termination meeting is to stay in control—to be the person who guides the progress of the meeting and determines what does and does not take place. By choosing what you say and how you say it, you can be firm and yet still show that the company cares.

Take a moment...

You have just informed Sam that he is being terminated because he has not improved his performance according to the agreed-upon plan. Sam begins to argue about it. In the space below, write down three different ways you can respond that show you practice the care and control approach to termination.

Step 3. Discuss the benefits and assistance that the company will provide

Once you've made the statement that the employee's job has been terminated and it has been briefly discussed, you can ask to move along with the meeting. In many companies, it is the human resources representative who takes over at this point to explain the benefits and assistance that the company will provide. It is important for the manager in charge of the termination discussion to remain in the meeting even if it is the HR representative who explains the assistance.

You can say something like:

"Roy, here is a letter that summarizes the benefits you will receive during your transition. Ed from human resources will go over this with you in more detail. If you have questions, you can contact Ed directly..."

The letter does not need to be lengthy, but it does need to explain the assistance that the company will provide. Here are two examples of effective letters. Note that the letter for a performance-related termination does not state the specific reason for the termination. Nothing is gained by reiterating the employee's performance shortfall in writing.

Sample letter for a termination due to downsizing

Date

John Doe
Home Address
City/State/ZIP Code

Dear John Doe:

This letter is to confirm our discussion of (date) and to summarize the benefits you will receive. Because of a downsizing, your position is one of several that has been eliminated.

To assist you in this transition, the company will provide:

1. XX weeks of salary continuance, based on our policy as stated in the Employee's Handbook.

2. A corresponding number of weeks of health insurance. You will be able to extend medical coverage after that period of time by paying the full premium. More information about this will be sent to you in the next two weeks.

3. A letter of reference that will be prepared by your manager in the next week.

4. Outplacement assistance to help you secure a new position.

In addition, you will receive payment for XX weeks of vacation accrued but not taken, according to our normal company policy.

Your contributions to the company are appreciated, and we want to provide whatever assistance we can during this transition. If you have further questions, please call me at 555-4567, ext. 7890.

Sincerely,

Manager

Sample letter for a termination due to poor performance

Date

John Doe
Home Address
City/State/ZIP Code

Dear John Doe:

This letter is to confirm our meeting of (date) and to summarize the benefits you will receive.

Your last day of employment with the ABC Corporation is (date). You will remove all personal belongings by (date) and return all company property by (date).

To assist you in your transition, the company will provide:

1. XX weeks of salary continuance, according to company policy.

2. Outplacement assistance.

In addition, you have XX weeks of vacation accrued, which will be paid to you in a lump sum according to company policy.

You have the option of purchasing health insurance under COBRA guidelines, and information is attached that explains the necessary procedures.

If you have any questions, please contact me.

Sincerely,

Manager

Having a letter on hand to review with the employee helps keep the discussion moving, provides the exiting employee with something to refer to the next day and makes it clear what the company will do and will provide. It is important, however, that this letter be prepared in advance and is ready to be given to the employee during the termination meeting. Use the examples just given as guidelines of what to include; each termination situation calls for its own unique summary letter. You will no doubt want to have your company's legal counsel review your letters.

Take a moment...

In the space below, write down three reasons why it is important to prepare a letter that summarizes the benefits and assistance that the company will provide the exiting employee.

_____

_____

_____

Step 4. Assist the employee in leaving the premises

As discussed in Chapter 2, there are two basic principles that should guide your decisions on this point: Do all you can to avoid embarrassing the exiting employee, and do all you can to avoid embarrassing remaining employees. These two guidelines will no doubt result in different procedures in different situations.

Unless the termination is due to gross misconduct, having security escort the exiting employee to the parking lot creates more problems than it solves. In general, you want to help the employee exit graciously and with as little notice as possible. You also want remaining employees to believe that you have treated the exiting employee fairly.

When outplacement specialists are on site, they can be of great assistance in helping the terminated employee exit the work site. Immediately after the termination discussion, introduce the exiting employee to the outplacement specialist(s). Let the outplacement person walk out of the building with the exiting employee. If any remaining employees observe the exit and ask questions, the manager can respond with something like: "Carol's position has been eliminated, and she has just left to begin her work with the outplacement people...."

That's a positive spin.

Should the terminated employee leave right after the termination meeting? Yes.

It is difficult for a person who has just been terminated to return to his or her work station and try to continue working. Put yourself in the other person's shoes: Could you be productive for several more hours if you had just been told that you'd lost your job?

If the exiting employee returns to his or her work station, even if just to retrieve personal articles, there will be questions, and disruption will follow. Even if it is for just a few items ("I only have two pictures and a plant on my desk..."), it usually is more effective to make arrangements for the employee to return after hours to pick up any personal belongings.

You can say something like: "Roy, we've learned what others have learned—that it's easier for you, and your co-workers, if you leave now. Let's make arrangements for you to return some evening or this weekend to get your personal belongings. We'll see that your work station is not disturbed."

Sometimes it's not easy to help the employee exit without some degree of embarrassment. If that's your situation, put into action procedures that will result in as little disruption as possible. Follow the rule of managing by common sense.

Self-check

Do you understand how to apply the care and control approach to termination when it comes time for the employee to leave the building? Complete the following exercises to find out. Suggested answers appear in the section beginning on page 109.

1. List two reasons why it's best not to have security escort the exiting employee to the door:

_____

_____

2. Indicate whether each of the following statements is True or False:

T/F   It is best to have the employee return to his or her workstation with a box and get personal belongings.

T/F   It is best to have security take a box to the exiting employee's workstation and remove what security believes are personal items.

T/F   It is best to ask some other employee who is a friend or who worked with the exiting employee to go and get the terminated employee's personal items.

3. Complete the sentence: The care and control approach to termination is to have the employee _____ to retrieve personal items.

Step 5. Document the termination meeting

After the termination meeting is completed and the employee has either exited the building or met with the outplacement specialist, take time to document the termination meeting. You and the other manager involved in conducting the meeting should prepare a brief summary of the session including what was said, the reactions and, in general, how the meeting progressed.

As you prepare this report, remember that its primary purpose is to serve as a chronicle of the meeting if, at some time in the future, the termination is called into question. This report is a document that can help you and the company respond to any intent to litigate the termination because it accurately summarizes what did and did not take place.

Both managers need to date and sign the report, and then file it in the appropriate places. Two examples of effective summary reports are given later in this chapter.

A sample script for a termination due to performance

Here is an example of how a termination for poor performance might progress:

Step 1. State the purpose of the meeting

Manager: Come in, Roy. Thank you for being prompt. I believe you know Todd from human resources. Let's sit at the table.

Employee: Why's Todd here? What's this meeting all about, anyway?

M: Roy, we've been working on your performance for the past two months. The company has provided some extra training for you, and you and I have set out some performance goals that we agreed were realistic. We also talked about what would happen if your performance didn't improve.

E: Wait a big minute here. My performance did improve!

Step 2. Guide and control the discussion

M: Yes, Roy, it did improve, but not to the level we agreed was realistic for you to attain.

E: But you never said I had to reach a certain level by a certain date.

M: Roy, please let me continue. We talked about what would happen if your performance didn't improve, and here are the notes from our several meetings. Our meeting today is to inform you that your employment with the ABC Corporation is terminated as of today and to tell you what the company will provide to assist you in this transition.

E: That's not fair! I was working hard to improve, and that's what really matters.

M: Roy, we talked earlier about performance levels, and you and I both agreed that they were realistic and that you could attain them. The improvement you did show was not enough; in fact, it was well below the goal we'd agreed on for this week.

E: Well, then, I want to talk with your boss. In fact, I want to talk with the president. He'll see that I get treated right.

M: Yes, my boss will be glad to talk with you, and when we're done with this meeting, we can call him to see when he will be available. He's aware of the termination, and so is the president. They both support the decision, and talking with them won't change it. But we can arrange it for you if that's what you'd like.

E: You bet it is.

Step 3. Discuss the benefits and assistance that the company will provide

M: Roy, let's move on with the meeting. Todd is here from human resources to explain the benefits and assistance that the company will provide.

(Todd explains the benefits, gives the employee the letter summarizing the benefits and talks about how and when the employee can remove his personal belongings.)

Step 4. Assist the employee in leaving the premises

M: Roy, we know you have some personal things at your workstation. One of the things we've learned over the years is that it will be easier on you as well as other employees if you come back after hours to pick those things up. Todd can meet you at the front desk today at 4:30 p.m. or tomorrow if that would work out better.

E: I just want to get out of here. Todd, I'll meet you tomorrow at 4:30.

M: As Todd said earlier, the company will provide outplacement assistance. And the person who will be helping you is here, waiting to meet with you and to get you started on a positive note for your transition. Let's go into the conference room to meet the outplacement specialist, and the two of you can leave together.

Step 5. Document the termination meeting

The manager and the human-resources representative stay and prepare a brief summary of the meeting:

On (date), we met with Roy Lastname to inform him of the termination of his employment because his performance had not improved to a previously agreed-upon level. Roy stated that his performance had improved, but (Manager) reminded him that his performance had not improved to the level both had agreed upon earlier. (Manager) also reminded Roy that he had been made aware of the consequences (termination) if his performance did not meet the agreed-upon level by this date. Roy asked to see (Manager's) boss and/or (CEO), and (Manager) stated that after the meeting, a call could be placed to see if either were available. (Manager) informed Roy that both were aware of the termination, that both had approved it and that the decision would not be changed by either individual. (Human Resources representative) gave Roy a letter summarizing the benefits and assistance Roy would receive and reviewed each item. Roy agreed to return tomorrow at 4:30 p.m. to retrieve his personal belongings from his workstation. The outplacement specialist was introduced, and Roy left the building with him.

(Signed by the Manager and the HR Representative)

A sample script for a termination due to downsizing

Here is an example of how a termination meeting that results from a downsizing might progress:

Step 1. State the purpose of the meeting

Manager: Thanks, Karen, for being so prompt for our meeting. I believe you know Ed from human resources. Let's sit around this table.

Employee: I don't think I know Ed. I'm glad to meet you. Have you been with the company long? How do you like it here?

M: Karen, I know it would be nice to take time to chat, but I think it's best for us if we get started with our meeting.

E: Sure, okay.

M: As you know, the company has been involved in cost-cutting efforts for the past year. Because of a reorganization to that end, there will be nine jobs eliminated today, and our meeting is to inform you that your job is one of them. We also want to tell you about what the company will be providing to help you in this transition.

E: I'm really surprised. I...I don't know what to say.

M: Yes, I...

E: But the more I think about it, the madder I get!

Step 2. Guide and control the discussion

M: I can....

E: In fact, I'm damn mad! I don't like this, and I want it changed! Who made this decision, anyway? I think it stinks. Is that why the new guy was brought in, to chop heads?

M: Karen, the decision was made by a reorganization team, who took many factors into consideration before they made their recommendations.

E: Yeah, well why don't you just tell me about it? Who else is getting the ax?

M: Karen, it really won't help at this point to talk about who else is leaving. What will help is for me to continue with our meeting and talk about the assistance the company will provide you during this transition.

E: Well, *you* may not want to talk about it, but I sure do. Who all was on this wonderful reorganization committee, anyway?

M: Karen, who served on the committee really doesn't matter now. The decision has been made, it's been approved all the way to the top, and it won't be reversed. Why don't we just continue with our meeting so I can tell you about the assistance you'll receive.

E: Big deal, big deal. I need a Kleenex. Do you have a Kleenex? Surely they issued you that as standard equipment....

M: Well, no they didn't, but I have some handy.

Step 3. Discuss the benefits and assistance to be provided

M: Ed is here from human resources to review the benefits and assistance you'll be receiving from the company.

(Ed presents the summary letter and goes through the information in more detail.)

E: You can say all you want—it's just going in one ear and out the other. I...I can't even remember what you just said.

HR Rep: That's alright. We understand, so we've prepared a summary letter you can look at later. Also, if you have any questions at all, please call me.

Step 4. Assist the employee in leaving the premises

M: Karen, we know you have personal items at your workstation. You can come back and get them this evening—or any other evening this week—or Saturday morning, if that would work best for you. We want to make it as easy for you as we can, and it seems to be easier for everyone else, too, to take care of this when there aren't so many around.

E: Yeah, well let me think about it. I still need to get my briefcase and my purse now, though.

M: That's fine, Karen, but first I'd like you to meet with one of the outplacement specialists who is here to talk with you briefly about what outplacement is and to get you scheduled for your first session. Then, when you collect your briefcase and your purse, it's probably best if you don't linger. The vice president of operations and I would like to personally tell the others in the work unit about this downsizing. We really appreciate your co-operation in this.

E: Yeah, yeah, I can do that. Hey, why would I want to stay?

Step 5. Document the termination meeting

The manager and the human resources representative sit down and jointly prepare the following report:

> On (date), we met with Karen Lastname and informed her of her employment termination with the ABC Corporation as of today due to downsizing. Karen asked several questions about who made the decision and why, and we informed her of the work of the reorganization committee. Karen was angry and made several sarcastic comments, but in general accepted the termination notice as well as could be expected. Ed informed her of the company's benefits and assistance and told her that she could call him directly with any questions. Karen said she would think about the best time to get her personal belongings and would let us know if it would be some evening this week or Saturday morning. We introduced her to the outplacement specialist.
>
> (Signed by the Manager and the HR Representative)

Does it ever really go like this? Sometimes, yes.

The key is to prepare and think through how you would like it to go. Anticipate the different employee reactions you might receive and how you will deal with each of them. As you think about what you will say and how you might react, keep the basic guidelines from Chapter 2 in mind, and the overall objective: care and control.

Chapter 4 review

Complete the following sentences. Suggested answers appear in the section beginning on page 109.

1. After you introduce the employee to the second manager present, you should tell the employee _____.

2. Sometimes you need to sound like a _____ if the employee wants to argue or discuss the termination decision.

3. When you discuss the assistance and benefits that the company will provide after the termination, it is very helpful to have_____.

4. The basic guideline to follow when the employee exits the premises is _____.

5. The termination meeting isn't over until you and the other manager _____.

Notes

Chapter 5

What do I do after the termination meeting?

Chapter 5 objectives

After reading this chapter and completing the interactive exercises, you should be able to:

➲ Complete your report documenting the termination meeting.

➲ Identify the best strategy for notifying other employees.

➲ Identify the best strategy for notifying affected customers of your company.

➲ Implement the transition of work duties.

➲ Describe how to handle reference checks.

➲ Determine how to handle future phone calls for the exiting employee.

"The termination meeting went well," Pam reported, "and Steve agreed to get his personal things from his office over the weekend. By the end of the week, though, it seemed like the whole place had fallen apart." Pam turned from staring out the window and continued. "Some of the people from Steve's work unit were getting pretty hostile toward their manager, and two customers called to cancel their orders. Obviously," Pam thought out loud, "we forgot something."

Right.

What Pam and her colleagues forgot were the necessary follow-up actions. These six tasks are often what makes the difference between a termination that results in minimal disruption and one that wreaks havoc.

Document the termination meeting

Though it was mentioned in the previous chapter, it's included again here so you won't forget it: Right after the termination discussion, you and the other person conducting the meeting need to sit down and draft a brief summary of the meeting. This report should summarize what was said, who said what and the general reactions. Then it should be signed by both managers, dated and placed in the appropriate files (one of these should be in human resources).

How detailed should you make this report? You should prepare the report in as much detail as you think will be necessary if, at some time in the future, the exiting employee comes back with a wrongful termination suit. The purpose of the report is to help you, and any others, recall the meeting if you ever need to defend your actions.

Notify other employees

Remaining employees know when a termination occurs, and they talk about it. They will talk about why it took place, whether they believe it was called for and whether they think the exiting employee was treated fairly. And there is nothing you can do to keep them from talking about it. What motivates all this attention? It's the unasked question, "What if that were me?" Employees want to know whether their co-worker's termination was justified and was handled well and if the exiting employee received some assistance in finding a new job.

The most effective way to help remaining employees assess the fairness of a co-worker's termination is to talk with them directly. This may take some extra time and energy, but it is part of maintaining control while you show that the company cares about its employees.

There are at least three positive results from talking directly with remaining employees:

1. Remaining employees will have accurate information, and questions, gossip or rumors won't take time from their other tasks.

2. If problems begin to develop among remaining employees, management can begin to deal with them before they get out of hand.

3. Management shows that it cares about its employees.

Here's how taking the time to explain the termination to your remaining employees demonstrates that you and your company care about them.

Notification of terminations due to performance

As quickly as possible after the termination meeting is concluded, the work unit's manager can inform the other work-unit employees about the termination. The announcement doesn't need to be lengthy, but it does need to take place very shortly after the termination takes place. This is best handled by the manager in charge of the work unit, with the unit's supervisor/manager assisting. Little detail needs to be provided; a simple statement seems to work best. You can say something like:

"We want to personally inform you that Bill's employment with us has been terminated, and this is his last day of work here. Bill already has left to return to his home to begin his job search. You might be interested in knowing that the company is providing the normal severance and outplacement assistance following the guidelines set out in the employee handbook."

Then the manager can briefly indicate who will be taking over Bill's responsibilities or how Bill's vacancy will be filled.

If one of the remaining employees asks, "Why?", it's best not to go into detail about the employee's failed performance but simply to respond with something like:

"Our policy, as you know, is not to talk in detail about why someone leaves. I wanted the work unit to hear about it from us as soon as it took place so you wouldn't hear it as a rumor or wonder where Bill is today."

If the exiting employee interfaced with other units, those units also should be told directly. If the exiting employee interfaced with units in other locations, those units need, at minimum, a phone call to announce the exit and to explain who will be taking over the responsibilities. If necessary, the remaining work units that had no direct contact with the exiting employee can be notified through a memo.

One of the things I've learned over the past 15 years in helping plan and conduct terminations is that the single most effective way to announce a termination to remaining employees is by direct, face-to-face contact with the appropriate managers. One of the most ineffective ways is by a general memo or a posting somewhere on a bulletin board.

Notification of terminations due to downsizing

It's important in a downsizing that upper-level managers are directly involved in telling the affected work units about the terminations. When Best Widget Corporation downsized, the president, Jim, met with each affected work unit to announce that several people from the unit had lost their jobs due to the downsizing. Jim also briefly described the severance and assistance each person would receive. Then he asked for questions.

"I took some verbal abuse," Jim said afterward, "and some anger certainly got directed my way. The next morning, however, several employees came by my office and told me that they appreciated the fact that the president came and made the announcement, not somebody else." Jim is certain that personally taking the time to make the announcement to each work unit was a major factor in minimizing disruption during the downsizing.

The announcement doesn't need to be long, but it needs to be personal and made directly to each affected work unit as quickly as possible after the termination meetings have been concluded.

Self-check

List three reasons why it is important to inform affected remaining employees about a termination. Suggested answers appear in the section beginning on page 109.

_____

_____

_____

Notify customers

If the terminated employee dealt directly with company customers, those key accounts need to be personally told of any change in who will be dealing with their accounts. Customers don't like continual changes in who handles their business, but they like it even less when they call for their account rep and receive the terse message, "We're sorry, but Cathy doesn't work here anymore."

When a termination is due to downsizing, it is even more important that key accounts be apprised of any changes. Depending on the account and the people involved, this can be done over the phone or in direct face-to-face meetings.

When the ABC Bank downsized, they analyzed all of the accounts handled by those who would be exiting. Then, while the termination meetings were taking place, several bank officers were out making personal calls on the affected accounts. In their meetings, the officers briefly talked about the downsizing and then explained who would be handling their accounts in the future.

"It took a lot of planning and legwork," bank executive Carole reported, "but we never lost any customers. In fact, because we took the time to personally inform our major accounts, other businesses were so impressed that they moved their accounts to our bank. We actually gained business, not lost it," she stated.

The least effective way to notify customers and key accounts is through a newsletter or mass mailing. Personalized letters sometimes work. But the most effective and caring approach with company customers is with:

- Direct contact, either by phone or a personal meeting.
- Contact by a company manager, officer or executive.
- Information that explains who will be handling the account.
- An introduction to the new person who will handle the account.

Companies consistently report that this direct contact with customers helps maintain or even enhances their standing in the marketplace!

Self-check

Bill's termination as part of a reorganization meant that some customers would be dealing with a different customer-service rep. Bill was well-liked, and customers enjoyed working with him. You want the transition to be as smooth as possible. Use the space below to outline how you would notify Bill's accounts. Suggested answers appear in the section beginning on page 109.

Implement the transition

Implementing the transition of job duties and responsibilities can begin as soon as the termination meeting is over and the affected remaining employees and customers have been notified. This transition usually is coordinated by the manager and supervisor of the specific work unit.

If the position was eliminated through a downsizing, those job duties usually are divided up among several other employees within the work unit. If the position will remain unfilled while a successor is recruited and hired, someone still needs to take care of those essential responsibilities. If there is no need to assign the exited employee's responsibilities to someone else, then there may be no need to fill the position at all, and you and your company have just reduced your overhead.

Reference checks

You should review your company's policy on providing references for exiting employees and identify the one person who will provide any reference information on the exiting employee(s). Companies are increasingly adopting the policy of providing no further information on former employees other than dates of employment and titles.

Often, companies that call to inquire about a former employee are referred to the human resources department for more information. When such calls come in, managers and supervisors are advised to transfer or refer the caller to human resources.

Otherwise, there can be problems. When the Reliable Widget Corporation was ready to offer Ted a new position, one of Reliable's managers said he knew someone from Ted's old company. A call was made to the company, and a manager there reported that Ted had trouble supervising people. Reliable Widget Corporation quickly changed its mind and didn't offer Ted the job. The information, however, was false; in fact, Ted had been commended several times for his ability to manage small groups. The manager from Ted's old company was disciplined, and the company volunteered to compensate Ted for "this mistake." But what Ted really wanted was the new job.

Some companies have taken this a step further and use a reference release. This is simply a form that the exiting employee signs that indicates what information the company can and cannot release to anyone who makes an inquiry. Even though this form can be reviewed and signed as part of the termination discussion, it's probably best to ask the employee to return it at a later date. That way, you avoid any possibility that the employee may feel pressured to sign it.

Example of a reference release

Employee Reference Release

I, _____ _____, agree to the release of the following information concerning my employment with (Company), as may be requested by prospective employers:

Job Reference Information	May Be Released	May Not Be Released
1. Dates of employment	_____	_____
2. Job title(s)	_____	_____
3. Salary at time of termination	_____	_____
4. Attendance record	_____	_____
5. Performance-review ratings	_____	_____

6. Reason for termination

__ Resignation
__ Resignation by mutual agreement
__ Retirement
__ Downsizing
__ Discharged for_____
__ Other (be specific)_____

7. Eligible for rehire

__ Yes
__ No

8. Other information that may be requested (be specific)

Signed:

Employee _____

Manager _____

Be sure to have your company legal counsel review and approve any form like this before putting it into use.

Take a moment...

Briefly describe your company's policy on providing references on former employees.

Is this policy outlined in the employee handbook?

_____

_____

_____

Is it consistent with good human resource practices?

_____

Does it show that the company cares about its employees?

_____

Messages

When the exiting employee is a manager or supervisor, has dealt with the consuming public or has been active in professional or community activities, he or she may continue to receive phone calls. Arrangements need to be made so that the receptionist does not give the terse "Alice doesn't work here anymore" message.

What works best is for calls to be transferred to some appropriate manager or administrative assistant who has been trained to deal with them. The caller can be told: "Alice is no longer with the ABC Corporation. If this is company-related, I can transfer you to the person who is now handling that area. Or if this has to do with some other professional or personal matter, I can see that Alice gets your message today."

Follow-through is essential.

Remember that your company is evaluated by every person who calls and asks for a terminated employee. If the caller is dealt with professionally and courteously, your company's image is enhanced. If not, you and your company's images are diminished.

Chapter 5 review

Here are the six follow-through activities you need to complete after a termination. Write down the actions you will take to carry them out.

1. Complete your report.

_____

_____

2. Tell the remaining employees.

_____

_____

3. Notify affected consumers of your product or service.

_____

_____

4. Implement the transition of work duties.

_____

_____

5. Respond to reference checks on the exited employee.

_____

_____

6. Respond to phone calls for the exited employee.

_____

_____

Notes

Chapter 6
What if...?

Chapter 6 objectives

After reading this chapter and completing the interactive exercises, you should know specific strategies for dealing with an employee who:

➲ Cries.

➲ Gets angry.

➲ Doesn't say anything.

➲ Insists on seeing your boss.

➲ Won't leave the building.

➲ Becomes physical.

➲ Is involved in gross misconduct.

"When Floyd started crying," Ed recalled, "I just plain didn't know what to do. So I just sat there wondering what was going to happen next..."

Despite our best planning, sometimes things happen that are out of the ordinary. Sometimes employees cry, even those who you'd least expect to react that way. Sometimes they just sit and won't say anything. And yes, once in a great while, someone gets really angry. Here are some suggestions for dealing with these and other special situations.

What if the employee cries?

Some employees become emotional after hearing of their termination, whether it's for performance reasons or due to a downsizing. They respond by crying. If you think the employee might cry, be prepared: Have some tissues on hand and within easy reach.

The best way to respond is to merely sit back for a few moments and let the person cry. This may be uncomfortable for you and the other person conducting the termination meeting, but you can handle it. Just how long do you wait for the employee to regain composure? That depends.

Most people will begin to regain their composure after just a few minutes. When you start to see this happen, you can say something like, "I know this isn't an easy time for you. But if you're ready, let's move on with our meeting and let me go over the severance assistance the company is going to provide for you..."

If the employee is ready, move on with the meeting. Bring out the letter that summarizes the severance and benefits, review it with the individual, and continue with the meeting.

If the employee continues to cry for several minutes and you're beginning to wonder when it will stop, you may need to be more assertive in regaining control of the meeting. Remember, however, that while you regain control, you must continue to show that the company cares.

Often, just repeating your message about continuing with the meeting is enough to bring the person out of shock. Sometimes the message needs to be repeated several times, firmly and controlled, but with a caring tone. Once in a great while, those conducting the termination meeting have found it necessary to ask if the person needed a few minutes to be alone. Then, the two people excuse themselves from the room, return later and say something like:

"We know this is not an easy situation, but, (first name), we believe it will be the most helpful if we can continue with the meeting. There is some important information we need to briefly review with you, and then you can have time to yourself. Let me tell you what the company will be doing to help you during this transition..."

You may believe the stereotype that it is only women who cry when told of a job termination. Wrong! The several people with whom I've worked who cried the most intensely and for the longest time were all male executives. Sometimes the employee who cries is the one you would least expect to respond in that way.

The key is not to become so embarrassed that you say or do inappropriate things at this awkward time. Remember, you need to show that the company cares—and you must remain in control of the meeting.

Self-check

You and the human resources manager are getting ready to tell Harold of his job elimination. You both think he might react by crying. Write down three things you can do in that event to conduct the meeting with care and control. Suggested answers appear in the section beginning on page 109.

_____

_____

_____

What if the employee becomes angry?

Unfortunately, people seem to be less in control of their anger today than they were even 10 years ago. You may encounter some anger that is directed not only at the company, but at you as its messenger.

It's important not to get pulled into the same kind of behavior and return anger with anger. If the employee's anger begins to move from verbal to physical, you obviously need to take preventive action. That is another reason always to have at least two people present during a termination meeting: It's more difficult for the exiting employee to be aggressively hostile if he or she has to confront two representatives of the company.

You can attempt to let the employee spout off and vent his or her anger but still must stay in control. And part of maintaining control means continuing to demonstrate that the company cares about the individual. After the employee has vented his or her anger, you can say something like:

"Roy, your anger may be a normal reaction, but it won't change things. The company does care about you, and we will be providing some assistance during this transition. Let's move on with our meeting so I can go over with you what this assistance includes..."

There are three very important guidelines to keep in mind:

1. Don't argue. If you begin to argue, you might say things that shouldn't be said, and you only serve to fuel the exiting employee's anger.

2. Don't respond in anger. If you respond in anger, you've not only demonstrated to the exiting employee that you have lost control of the meeting but, more importantly, that you and the company may not really care about your people.

3. Stay in control. Take a few deep breaths. Keep your voice calm. Don't raise your pitch. Look to the other person helping conduct the meeting for assistance.

If you lose control and respond in anger, the exiting employee has won, and his or her anger will have paid off in wresting control of the meeting from you. Whatever you say must be said in a calm and "in-charge" manner.

Sometimes the person in charge of the termination discussion becomes so involved in trying to deal with the terminated employee's anger that he or she doesn't react well. This is when the second person, who usually is more of an observer up to this point, can step in with the right words or actions to help defuse the employee's anger.

If you think you will have to deal with an angry employee, prepare yourself. Anticipate what the soon-to-be-terminated employee might say or do, and talk with your meeting partner about how each of you might react.

Preparation is important. And so is control.

Self-check

Write down three things you can do if an employee becomes angry during the termination meeting. Suggested answers appear in the section beginning on page 109.

_____

_____

_____

What if the employee doesn't say anything?

Sometimes employees are so in shock at hearing that their employment has been terminated that they just sit and stare into space. As with an employee who cries, you can sit in silence for a few moments. Then you have to make a decision: Is the person in shock, or has the person just plain tuned you out?

You can say something like this:

"Roy, let's move on with the meeting. There are some things we need to go over together now, and then you can have some time of your own to sit and think."

If the person doesn't respond and continues to stare into space, you may need to repeat your statement, except this time perhaps a little more loudly. You also can give emphasis to the exiting employee's name and even repeat it several times.

Remember, though, don't panic. The person soon will regain composure and you can continue with your meeting. What are your basic guidelines? Care and control.

Self-check

David seems to be in total shock. He doesn't say anything, and he just sits and stares into space. Here are five possible actions you could take. Which two are the most appropriate?

1. You continue to sit and wait until David finally says something.

2. You sit quietly for a few moments, and then ask David if the two of you can continue with the meeting.

3. You bang your fist on the table to get David's attention.

4. You grab David by the shoulders and give him a good shake.

5. You repeat David's name and your request to continue with the meeting.

The manager who uses the care and control approach to termination would choose the second and fifth actions.

What if the employee wants to see your boss?

Sometimes an employee may insist on seeing your boss or even the CEO. "When Sharon hears about what you just did to me, she'll reverse it," the exiting employee might say.

It's best if you go ahead and make arrangements for the terminated employee to see your boss or an upper-level executive. Make it clear, however, that you will agree to do this only after your discussion is completed. And remind the employee that these senior-level people are aware of the termination decision, have approved it and will not reverse it based on these subsequent meetings.

You can say something like:

"Roy, I'm sure that Bob will see you after we're through with our meeting. But we have to complete our meeting first. You should know that Bob is aware of your termination and already has given his approval. The decision will not be changed. But if you still want to see him when we're through, we can call his office to set up an appointment."

The key, of course, is that the upper-management person indeed has been apprised of the termination and supports the decision. No senior-level executive ever should reverse a termination decision based on the plea of the exiting employee. That merely sets a precedent for every employee who is terminated in the future to follow.

Self-check

Ted's job was eliminated as part of a reorganization. A long-term employee, Ted, and several company executives, including your boss, take a Canadian fishing trip each spring. You expect that Ted will demand to see your boss in an attempt to get the job elimination reversed. What are three things you can do that follow the care and control approach to termination? Suggested answers appear in the section beginning on page 109.

_____

_____

_____

What if the employee won't leave the building?

"We talked about Sam's coming back this evening to get the things from his office," Leigh said, "but all he did was go back to his work area and talk with the others. He really caused quite a commotion," Leigh continued, "and nobody got much done for the rest of the day. Trouble was, that unit had some important reports to complete that were not ready on time."

It happens. Sometimes, even after the employee has agreed to leave, the exiting employee won't exit. He or she stays, and the longer the stay, the greater the disruption.

When that occurs, you need to be assertive and approach the exiting employee directly. You can take him or her aside and say something like:

"Sam, I really need to ask for your cooperation. Your staying and talking with the others is causing a lot of disruption, and you're making some people very uncomfortable. We talked about your leaving now, and I'm going to have to ask you to make good on your agreement to leave the building now."

What if he or she still won't go? You are left basically with just one option, and that is to call security and ask for assistance in escorting the employee to transportation. Of course, that is almost never a desirable scenario, but sometimes it's better than letting the exiting employee remain on the premises and create trouble.

One advantage of having the outplacement providers on site is that the exiting employee can then leave the building with them. The outplacement specialists should be sensitive to the need for the employee to leave the building directly and be ready to help ensure the person's exit.

Self-check

Cathy was always a good worker, even though she liked to talk a lot and sometimes kept others from getting their work done. After she was told of her termination due to a downsizing, Cathy said she'd leave the building and come back in the evening to clean out her desk. But instead she stayed. And stayed. And soon there were seven people standing around talking with Cathy. What are three things you could do to prevent further disruption? Suggested answers appear in the section beginning on page 109.

_____

_____

What if the employee becomes physical?

We've all read about how a very few terminated employees become violent and do something rash. If you expect that the exiting employee might turn hostile and physical, by all means, take precautions. First, be certain that the room in which you will be meeting has been "sanitized"—that is, you've removed any articles and objects that easily could be picked up and thrown. Second, have security on hand, apprised of the situation and prepared to help if needed. Third, be certain that at least two representatives of the company conduct the termination meeting. It is more difficult for an employee to become hostile and aggressive if more than one manager is present.

Finally, remain in control. If the exiting employee attempts to become physical, then, of course, protect yourself. But try to do so in a voice and manner that shows you are not frightened (even if you are), and that demonstrates you still are in control of the situation.

If you think the soon-to-be-terminated employee might become physically aggressive, seek specialized assistance from a local security agency or your police department. If you still wonder what to do, rely on the Rule of Common Sense: Do what makes sense to you.

The percentage of termination discussions that result in physical violence is very, very, small—a small fraction of a percent, at most.

If you plan carefully and have considered all aspects of the termination and the meeting, you probably will never have to deal with a physical reaction from a terminated employee.

Self-check

In the space below, write down four things you can do if you anticipate a physical reaction from an employee during the termination meeting. Suggested answers appear in the section beginning on page 109.

_____

_____

_____

_____

What if the employee is involved in gross misconduct?

Instances of gross misconduct call for special policies and procedures. First, gross misconduct should be defined in the company's employee handbook. Typically, it includes, but is not limited to, instances of fighting, willful recklessness, willful negligence, stealing and use of drugs on the job.

The following procedures are recommended for instances of gross misconduct:

1. Isolate the employee as soon as gross misconduct has been identified. Escort the employee to a conference room or the manager's office, where the employee will not have contact with other employees. You do not want the employee to have access to others in an effort to build sympathy or distort events.

2. Involve other decision-makers. With the employee isolated, the supervisor and appropriate managers can calmly review the situation, seek legal counsel if needed and make their decisions. Even if they decide to terminate the employee at that moment, they still must complete the appropriate paperwork prior to giving the termination notice. At least two decision-making levels of management always should be involved with any termination due to gross misconduct.

3. Document the decision. Even before the termination notice is given to the employee, the appropriate managers should prepare a written summary of the incident and their decision to terminate. It should be signed by all, with the date and time noted. Then, a second written summary should be prepared to document what happened during the termination meeting.

4. Terminate and escort. At least two people should be present to inform the employee of his or her termination, effective immediately. Typically, no severance is provided in terminations due to gross misconduct. A manager can gather personal items from the employee's workstation and then escort the employee to his or her transportation. If the employee

does not have transportation, the company can hire a cab to take the employee home.

It is important that emotion does not overtake reason or company policy in instances of gross misconduct. The basic guideline is: Act slowly, be thorough and involve other levels of management in the decision-making.

Self-check

Briefly describe how your company defines gross misconduct:

_____

_____

_____

Hal started a fight with his co-worker over who would go next for a 15-minute break. As the fight is broken up, you smell alcohol on Hal's breath. He's wobbly, verbally abusive and angry. What would you do? Suggested answers appear in the section beginning on page 109.

_____

_____

_____

_____

_____

_____

Chapter 6 review

You've just been given much information on how to conduct a variety of care and control terminations—even when the situation goes beyond "normal." Are you comfortable that you know how to deal with an employee who cries? Or one who doesn't say anything? How about the individual who won't leave the building? The following exercises can help you assess your readiness to deal with these special situations.

For each item below, take time to review your knowledge and comfort level in dealing with the special situation. Then, write down how you would handle it using the care and control approach to termination.

1. The employee begins to cry after I explain his or her termination.

_____

_____

2. The employee becomes angry and starts to shout at me and the other person conducting the termination.

_____

_____

3. The employee just sits and stares out the window and doesn't say a word.

_____

_____

4. The employee insists on seeing my boss—now!

_____

_____

5. The employee won't leave the building.

_____

_____

6. The employee starts to argue and then becomes physically aggressive.

_____

_____

Notes

Chapter 7

How do I put the care and control approach into action?

Chapter 7 objectives

After reading this chapter and completing the interactive exercises, you should be able to:

➲ Evaluate your readiness to apply the care and control approach to termination.

➲ Identify a plan for implementing the care and control approach to termination.

The care and control approach is by far the most effective termination procedure. When you put the care and control approach into action, you show that the company truly cares about its employees—even those who must exit. As you stay in control, you not only protect the company and the company's customers, but you also help make sure that the exiting employee doesn't do or say anything he or she will later regret.

The result?

● The exiting employee retains his or her self-esteem in the transition process.

● The exiting employee leaves with regard for the company.

● The risk of litigation is reduced.

● The company is regarded as a good place to work by remaining employees.

● Potential employees think of the company as a good place to work.

● The company's reputation in the marketplace is now enhanced.

That's a lot of results!

Throughout this book, you've learned about the care and control approach to termination. You've learned what care involves and how to stay in control. Now you're ready to put all of this into action.

Take a moment...

The care and control approach to termination is built upon learning several basic guidelines and applying these guidelines to the many situations you may encounter. These guidelines and their applications are summarized in the following statements. Take time now to honestly evaluate your readiness to implement the care and control approach.

1=I'm ready   2=I need more preparation

___ I understand the benefits of the care and control approach to termination.

___ I understand why business decisions sometimes result in terminations.

___ My own role in the care and control approach to termination is clear to me.

___ My words and actions in a termination meeting will show that the company cares about its employees—even those who must exit.

___ I can begin the termination discussion without socializing.

___ I can remain in control of the termination discussion even if the employee argues.

___ I know how to plan and conduct the termination without causing undue embarrassment to the exiting employee.

___ I know how to plan and conduct the termination without causing undue embarrassment to the remaining employees.

___ I know the three reasons why it's important always to have at least two people conduct the termination discussion.

___ I understand that protecting the company's customers sometimes necessitates terminations.

___ I am able to review the reasons for a termination and to determine if sufficient documentation exists.

___ I know why it is best to schedule the termination meeting early in the week and early in the day.

___ I understand that there are several very important reasons why Friday afternoon is the worst time for a termination meeting.

___ I can prepare a script or outline of what I will say during the termination meeting.

___ I am familiar with the logistics outlined in the termination planning guide and know how to coordinate them for a care and control approach to termination.

___ I know what to include in a summary report of the termination discussion, and how to file it appropriately.

___ I can plan the most effective way to help an employee leave the premises.

___ Notifying other employees is an integral part of my care and control approach.

___ Notifying company customers of an employee's exit is part of my care and control approach (as appropriate).

___ I can explain to others how to handle reference checks.

___ I can explain to others how to handle phone calls for the exited employee.

___ I know how to use the care and control approach in dealing with an employee who:

- Cries.

- Becomes angry.

- Argues.

- Doesn't say anything.

- Wants to see my boss.

- Won't leave the building.

- Becomes physically aggressive.

- Is involved in gross misconduct.

___ I believe in the care and control approach and am ready to put it into practice!

Review your responses to the exercise you just completed. For any aspects of the care and control approach to termination that you rated as needing more preparation, turn to the appropriate sections and reread the information. Be sure to take time to rethink the exercises and interact with them again, too.

Remember that the detailed termination planning guide is located in the back of this book for your future reference.

Putting words into action

Congratulations! You've finished the book, and are ready to put its words into action. You're ready to implement the care and control approach to termination. Now you need just one more element—commitment:

- Commitment to the belief that the care and control approach is the *best* approach to termination.

● Commitment to devote the time and effort necessary to bring the care and control approach to reality.

● Commitment that the care and control approach to termination will become your standard of excellence.

Once you make these commitments, you're truly ready to put the care and control approach into practice. Your words will become actions. You will be ready for any situation because you understand two very basic guidelines:

Care: You do everything you can to show that the company cares about its employees, even an employee who has been terminated.

Control: You do everything you can to remain in control of the situation.

That's the care and control approach to termination!

10 tips for putting the care and control approach into action

1. Take time to review the termination situation to ensure that all company policies are being followed.

2. Take time to prepare your script—your outline of what you plan to say.

3. Anticipate how the employee might react to the termination, and plan how you will respond.

4. Always include at least one other supervisor or manager to assist you during the termination meeting.

5. Conduct the termination discussion at a time and in a place where both the employee and the remaining employees will not be unduly embarrassed.

6. Identify a way to exit the building that will cause the least embarrassment to the employee and the remaining employees.

7. Always prepare a brief summary report of the termination meeting and file it appropriately.

8. Take time to notify remaining employees and, when appropriate, affected company customers.

9. Use the termination planning guide (in back) to review your entire planning process.

10. Remember always to think care and control.

Notes

Answers to selected exercises

Chapter 1

Self-check (page 21)

The first and seventh statements are False. The rest are True.

Chapter 3

Self-check (page 45)

Karen's supervisor demonstrated the care and control approach to termination by ensuring that these six things were done:

1. Poor performance had been noted, complete with dates when performance was not up to standards.

2. She had made performance expectations clear to Karen.

3. Both Karen and her supervisor had signed the reports summarizing their various meetings together.

4. Efforts to provide help for Karen had been documented.

5. Karen knew the consequences of not meeting the performance expectations.

6. All company policies had been followed.

Chapter review (page 52-53)

1. The five basic planning steps for any termination meeting are:

   ● Review the reasons for the termination.

   ● Schedule the meeting.

   ● Prepare your script.

   ● Coordinate logistics.

   ● Plan for follow-through.

2. Statements 3, 5 and 6 are True.

3. The following all are logistics items that must be coordinated:

   ● The termination has been reviewed and approved.

   ● The meeting room has been scheduled.

   ● The employee will be available at the time of the meeting.

   ● A second person to assist in the meeting is available.

   ● A script has been prepared and reviewed with the second person.

   ● A summary letter for the employee will be ready at the time of the meeting.

   ● Options for removal of the employee's personal belongings have been approved.

Chapter 4

Self-check (page 64)

1. Two reasons it's best not to have security escort the employee to the door are:

   ● It causes undue embarrassment to the exiting employee.

● It causes undue embarrassment to the remaining employees.

2. All of the statements are False.

3. The care and control approach to termination is to have the employee return to the workplace after hours or on the weekend to retrieve personal items.

Chapter review (page 72)

1. After you introduce the employee to the second manager present, you should tell the employee *the purpose of the meeting*.

2. Sometimes you need to sound like a *broken record* if the employee wants to argue or discuss the termination decision.

3. When you discuss the assistance and benefits that the company will provide after the termination, it is very helpful to have *a letter for the employee summarizing the assistance and benefits the company will provide*.

4. The basic guideline to follow when the employee exits the premises is *to do all you can to avoid embarrassing the employee as well as the remaining employees*.

5. The termination meeting isn't over until you and the other manager *prepare a brief summary of the meeting, sign it and file it appropriately*.

Chapter 5

Self-check (page 80)

Three reasons it is important to inform affected remaining employees about a termination are:

1. Remaining employees will receive accurate information, and rumors won't take time from their job tasks.

2. If problems begin to develop among remaining employees, management can begin to deal with them before they get out of hand.

3. Management shows that it cares about its employees.

Self-check (page 81)

You will notify Bill's accounts personally and directly—either through a phone call or a face-to-face meeting on the same day that the downsizing occurs. You will want to make this contact before the customers hear about the downsizing through the media or from some other company.

Chapter 6

Self-check (page 90)

1. Let Harold cry for a few moments, express concern, then redirect him to the meeting at hand when he calms down.

2. If he continues to cry, repeat the message about getting back to the meeting.

3. If Harold still cries, allow him a few minutes alone, then continue with the meeting.

Self-check (page 92)

1. Don't argue.

2. Don't respond in anger.

3. Look to the other person helping conduct the meeting for assistance.

Self-check (page 94)

1. Make arrangements for Ted to see your boss.

2. Make it clear you will only do this after your discussion with Ted is completed.

3. Remind Ted that your boss has already approved the termination decision and will not reverse it.

Self-check (page 95)

1. Remind Cathy she is causing disruption and ask her directly to leave the building.

2. Have on-site placement providers leave the building with Cathy.

3. Ask for assistance from security in escorting Cathy to transportation if she continues to stay.

Self-check (page 96)

1. Remove from the meeting room any articles or objects that could be picked up and thrown easily.

2. Have security on hand.

3. Have at least two company representatives conduct the termination meeting.

4. Remain in control.

Self-check (page 98)

1. Isolate Hal as soon as his misconduct is known.

2. Involve other managers or supervisors in the decision to terminate.

3. Document the decision to terminate

4. Terminate and escort.

Termination planning guide

This guide has been designed to help you think through the issues and logistics for termination or downsizing. Though each item may not apply to every situation, it is important that you respond to each line. When you have provided the information called for, check the box for each section so that you know it has been considered and the appropriate planning is done. Your planning is not completed until all items have been checked.

Confidential

For use by

_____

Supervisor/Manager

Termination planning guide

This guide has been designed to help you think through all of the issues and areas of concern for both single terminations and downsizings. Respond to each item. As you complete the planning for each item, place a check mark or your initials in each box.

Termination planning guide

☐ **1. Employee Information**

Name: _____

Title: _____

Age: _____ Years with company: _____

Salary: _____

Names/titles of any relatives working for the company: ____

_____

Member of any protected class of employee:_____

Days/hours of unused accrued vacation, and method of compensation: _____

_____

Other: _____

☐ **2. The Termination Decision**

Reason for termination: _____

What the employee will be told: _____

If due to performance: _____

Documentation reviewed: _____ _____

By whom: _____

Notes on documentation and possible risks: _____

If due to job elimination:

Criteria established and approved:_____

By whom: _____

Others within the employee's work unit whose jobs also are being eliminated: _____

_____

☐ **3. Assistance to Be Provided**

Length of salary continuance (severance): _____

Outplacement services and objectives for outplacement: ____

_____

Insurance benefits (specific):_____

Other special considerations: _____

How will the employee be notified of COBRA options?:_____

_____

Will unemployment be allowed/contested?: _____

☐ **4. The Termination Meeting**

Date/time: _____

Location:_____

To be conducted by (names and titles of at least two people):

_____

_____

Will a letter summarizing benefits be ready?: _____

Will outplacement be conducted on-site?: _____

   If so, where?:_____

Has a room been scheduled for the outplacement specialists?:

_____

What will the employee be told? (outline of the proposed script):_____

_____

How/when will the employee remove any personal belongings?:

_____

Supervised by: _____

Other special considerations: _____

_____

☐ 5. The Employee's Future Employment

If the termination is due to job elimination:

Has the employee been considered for other openings within the company?: _____

Will the employee be considered for any future positions within the company?: _____

How will the company notify the employee of future job postings?: _____

How will references be handled?: _____

By whom?: _____

Will a general letter of reference be prepared?: _____

By whom?: _____

When will it be available?: _____

Will the employee be asked to sign and return a reference release form?: _____

☐ 6. Internal Communications

What will the work unit be told?: _____

By whom?: _____

When?: _____

What will phone callers be told?: _____

By whom?: _____

☐ **7. External Communications**

Key customers, salespeople, vendors and others who may be affected by the employee's exit: _____

_____

How will these people be notified of the change in personnel?:

_____

By whom?: _____

When?: _____

Will the media be involved?: _____

If so, who will be the single person assigned to deal with the media?: _____

What will the media be told?: _____

Will a press release be prepared?: _____

About the author

Richard S. Deems, Ph.D., is the founder and CEO of Deems Associates Inc., a national career-management consulting firm. For nearly 20 years, Dr. Deems has helped thousands of people across this country and in Canada prepare to interview for jobs with confidence.

In *Hiring: More Than a Gut Feeling*, Deems presents a step-by-step system to help decision-makers implement effective hiring decisions—decisions based on *more than a gut feeling*.

Deems received his bachelor's degree from Nebraska Wesleyan University, his master's degree from Northwestern University, and his Ph.D. from the University of Nebraska at Lincoln, with an emphasis in adult development.

He is the author of numerous articles on career-management issues, and is frequently quoted as an expert in the career-management field. Deems also is the author of *Hiring: More Than A Gut Feeling*.

Index

Age, 45-46
Aggression, 35
Anger, 35, 49, 59
Angry employee, dealing
    with, 90-92
Arguing, 14, 28, 31-32, 35, 49,
    58-59
Assistance, in transition
    process, 13, 23
Attracting top-level
    employees, 19-20, 29

Benefits and assistance, 60-63,
    67, 70
Bias, 45-46
Business decisions, 23-24

Care and control approach, 13-15,
    18, 21-22, 47-49, 102-107
Career counseling, 23
Caring, 29, 78
Commitment to care and control
    approach, 105-106
Company
    employees' regard for, 18-20,
      29, 102
    policies, 43-45, 50, 82, 97-98
    reputation, 13, 19-20, 22, 29, 85,
      102

Conducting the termination
    meeting, 56-71
Control, 14, 29
Coordinating logistics, 50-51
Crying employee, dealing
    with, 88-90
Customers
    informing, 14, 37, 47-48, 80-81
    protecting, 28, 36-37

Delaying termination, 44
Dignity, retaining, 13
Disabilities, 45
Discrimination, 17-18, 45-46
Disruption, 13-14, 28, 34, 64
Documentation, 43-45, 50, 58,
    65-66, 68, 71, 77, 97
Downsizing, 18, 22-24, 36, 45-46,
    48, 57, 61, 68-71, 79-81
Drug use on the job, 97

Embarrassment, avoiding, 13-14,
    28-29, 32-34, 48, 63-64
Employees
    attracting top-level, 19-20, 29
    informing other, 14, 33-34,
      47-48, 77-78
    morale of, 29
    poor-performing, 23, 36